GHOSTS
THE UNSOLVED MYSTERY

BY LISA WADE McCORMICK

Reading Consultant:
Barbara J. Fox
Reading Specialist
North Carolina State University

Content Consultant:
Andrew Nichols, PhD
Executive Director
American Institute of Parapsychology
Gainesville, Florida

Capstone

Mankato, Minnesota

Blazers is published by Capstone Press,
151 Good Counsel Drive, P.O. Box 669, Mankato, Minnesota 56002.
www.capstonepress.com

Library of Congress Cataloging-in-Publication Data
McCormick, Lisa Wade, 1961–
    Ghosts: the unsolved mystery/ by Lisa Wade McCormick
    p. cm. — (Blazers. Mysteries of Science)
    Includes bibliographical references and index.
    Summary: "Presents the study of ghosts, including current theories and famous examples" — Provided by publisher.
    ISBN-13: 978-1-4296-2327-8 (hardcover)
    ISBN-10: 1-4296-2327-6 (hardcover)
    1. Ghosts — Juvenile literature. I. Title. II. Series.
BF1461.M42 2009
133.1 — dc22   2008028699

Editorial Credits
Lori Shores, editor; Alison Thiele, designer; Marcie Spence, photo researcher

Photo Credits
Alamy/Dale O'Dell, 24–25, 27; Dennis Hallinan, 26; Gary Doak, cover;
    Mary Evans Picture Library, 10–11
Fortean Picture Library, 4–5, 14–15
Getty Images Inc./Michael O'Leary, 28–29
iStockphoto/Gregory Spencer, 22
Landov LLC/Jessica Rinaldi/Reuters, 18–19; Marvin Fong/Newhouse News Service, 20–21
Mary Evans Picture Library, 6, 7, 8–9
Newscom/Jupiter Images, 12–13; Nam Y. Huh/South Florida Sun-Sentinel, 23
Shutterstock/Marilyn Volan, grunge background (throughout); Maugli, 16–17 (background);
    rgbspace, (paper art element) 3, 17; Shmeliova Natalia, 16 (paper art element)

TABLE OF CONTENTS

CHAPTERS

A Haunting . . . .

Ghost Stories 5

Ghost Hunting 11

Are Ghosts Real? 18

. . . . 25

FEATURES

Famous Ghosts . . . .

Glossary 16

Read More 30

Internet Sites 31

Index 31

. . . . 32

GHOST FACT

Spooky noises are often heard in haunted places. Some people have heard crying. Others have heard laughter.

A HAUNTING

Strange moans echoed through the **haunted** building. Whispers came from the walls. "Don't Carlos, don't."

haunted — having mysterious events happen often, possibly due to ghosts

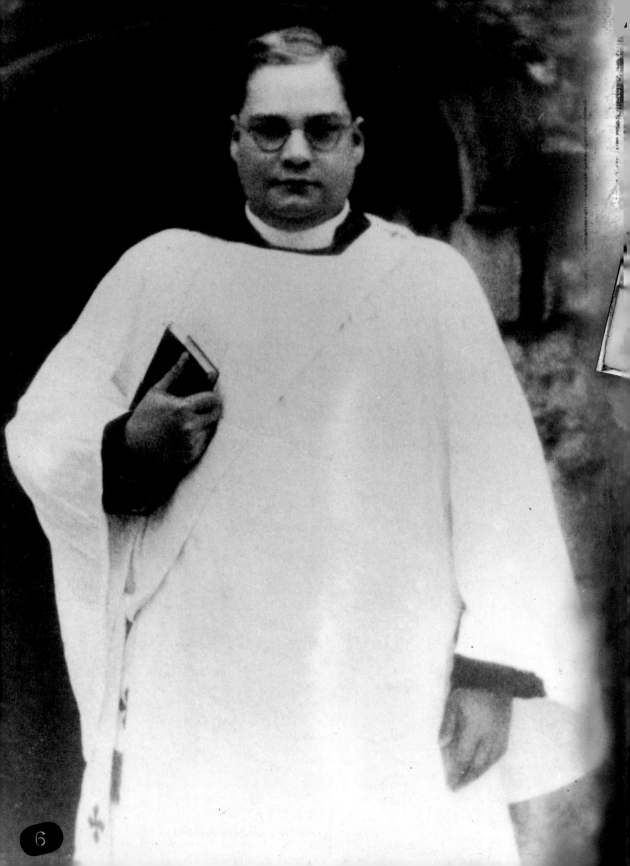

Writing appeared on the walls of Borley Rectory in 1930.

Reverend Guy Eric Smith heard the voices. He lived in the Borley **Rectory** in 1928.

rectory — a house where church leaders live

Who made the strange noises? Was it the cloudy figure that people saw at Borley Rectory? Or could the noises be explained in another way?

Borley Rectory was known as the most haunted house in England. The building burned down in 1939.

drawing room of the Borley Rectory

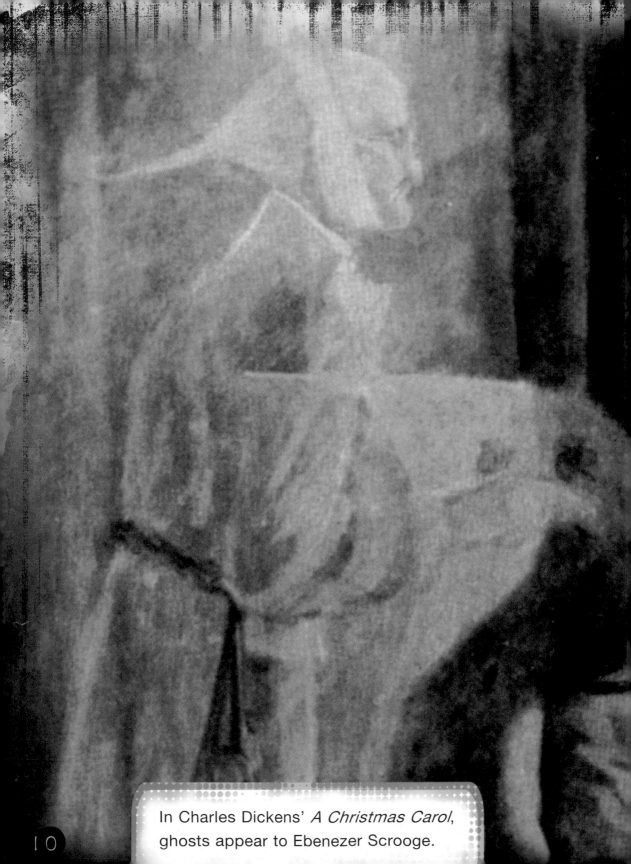

In Charles Dickens' *A Christmas Carol*, ghosts appear to Ebenezer Scrooge.

GHOST STORIES

Ghost stories are told around the world. These tales have scared people for thousands of years.

Many people think ghosts are **spirits** of people who have died. These spirits may not be ready to leave this life. They may be angry or confused.

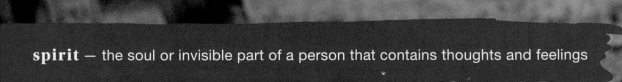

spirit — the soul or invisible part of a person that contains thoughts and feelings

GHOST FACT

Ghosts are sometimes seen where people have died. Many people have seen ghosts near battlefields.

Ghosts may appear as dark shadows or cloudy figures. Some people have seen ghosts of **deceased** family members or friends.

GHOST FACT

Some people believe they have seen ghosts of pets that have died.

deceased — dead

This picture of a burning building was taken in 1995. The ghost of a young girl seems to be standing in the doorway.

FAMOUS GHOSTS

Many people report seeing the ghost of former President Abraham Lincoln in the White House. Four presidents have seen his ghost. Workers and visitors say they have also seen the ghost.

Gettysburg, Pennsylvania, may be the most haunted place in the United States. Thousands of soldiers died there during the Civil War (1861–1865). Visitors report seeing ghostly soldiers on the battlefield.

Many ghost sightings have been reported on the cruise ship the *Queen Mary*. The ghost of a girl who drowned is seen near the pool. People say they have also seen the ghost of the ship's captain.

A ghost may have bothered the Bell family of Adams, Tennessee, in 1817. Family members said the ghost made noises outside their home. It later pulled blankets off beds. Twelve-year-old Betsy Bell said the ghost even slapped her.

GHOST HUNTING

Ghost hunting is a hobby to many people. There are scientists who study ghosts too. They try to understand ghosts and hauntings.

Ghost hunters often find simple reasons for ghostly sounds. The sounds can come from pipes or mice in the walls.

GHOST FACT

Ghost hunters work at night. They use cameras that take pictures in the dark.

Ghost hunters look for changes in a room's temperature. They say ghosts can make a room 10 degrees cooler.

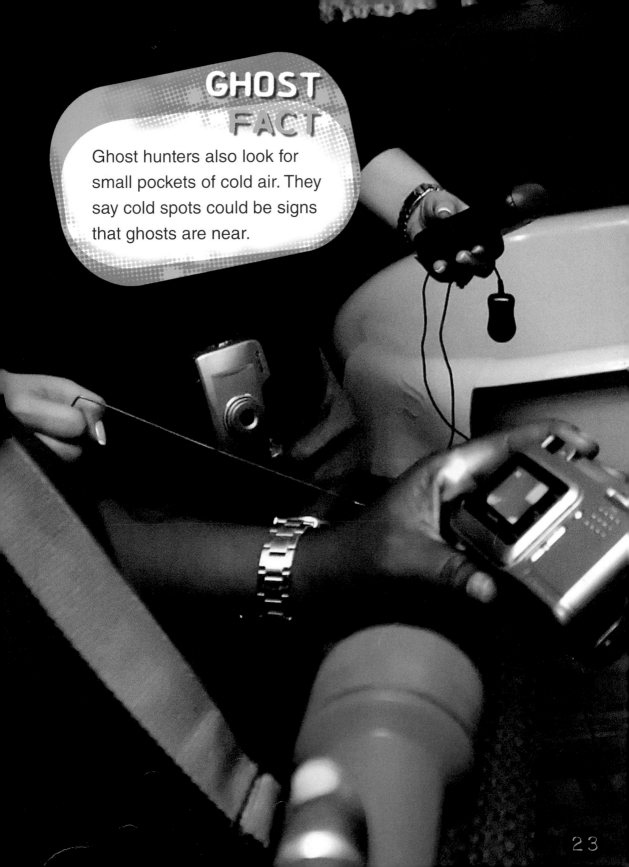

Ghost hunters also look for small pockets of cold air. They say cold spots could be signs that ghosts are near.

ARE GHOSTS REAL?

Many scientists don't believe in ghosts. They say there is no **proof**. Many pictures of ghosts have turned out to be fakes.

proof — facts that show something is true

25

But many ghost hunters say there is proof. They say temperature changes and recorded voices prove ghosts are real.

GHOST FACT

Ghostly voices caught on tape are called Electronic Voice Phenomena, or EVP.

Are the findings of ghost hunters enough proof? Or are there other reasons for these strange events? That is the mystery ghost hunters hope to solve.

GHOST FACT

According to a survey done in 2007, one-third of Americans believe in ghosts.

Some people have reported seeing ghosts in graveyards.

GLOSSARY

deceased (di-SEEST) — dead

haunted (HAWN-ted) — having mysterious events happen often, possibly due to visits from ghosts

proof (PROOF) — facts that show something is true

rectory (REK-tuh-ree) — a house or building where church leaders live

spirit (SPIHR-it) — the soul or invisible part of a person that is believed to control thoughts and feelings; some people believe the spirit leaves the body after death.

READ MORE

Gee, Joshua. *Encyclopedia Horrifica: The Terrifying Truth! About Vampires, Ghosts, Monsters, and More.* New York: Scholastic, 2007.

Pipe, Jim. *Ghosts.* Tales of Horror. New York: Bearport, 2007.

Teitelbaum, Michael. *Famous Ghosts.* Chanhassen, Minn.: Child's World, 2007.

INTERNET SITES

FactHound offers a safe, fun way to find educator-approved Internet sites related to this book.

Here's what you do:

1. Visit *www.facthound.com*
2. Choose your grade level.
3. Begin your search.

This book's ID number is 9781429623278.

FactHound will fetch the best sites for you!

INDEX

battlefields, 13, 16
Bell family, 17
Borley Rectory, 7, 8, 9

Electronic Voice
    Phenomena (EVP),
    27

Gettysburg, Pennsylvania,
    16
ghost hunting, 18, 20, 22,
    23, 26, 28
ghost stories, 11

Lincoln, President
    Abraham, 16

noises, 4, 8, 17, 20

pets, 14
pictures, 25

Queen Mary, 17

scientists, 18, 25
Smith, Reverend Guy
    Eric, 7
spirits, 12

temperature, 22, 26

voices, 4, 5, 7, 26

White House, 16